a THIN Book of Fat Poems

10-15-18

To Dear Louise,

Some people have "angel" written all over their face. You are one of the angels that brought some light into my heart.

Thank you,

With God's Love

a THIN Book of **Fat** Poems

A THIN BOOK of Fat POEMS

ARTPEACE
PUBLISHING

a THIN BOOK of **Fat** POEMS

For my beloved, late father Zdzisław Przewłócki, Ph.D., whose unconditional love, resourcefulness, selfless heart, humility, strength, and humor enabled me to get through my very hardest times.

A THIN BOOK OF FAT POEMS
Copyright © 2016 by Liliana Kohann
Cover Drawing and Design © 2016 by Liliana Kohann
ISBN: 978-1-945453-00-7

Published by ARTPEACE PUBLISHING
Nashville, TN, USA in 2016.
All rights reserved. No part of this book may be reproduced by any manner whatsoever without written permission, except in the case of brief quotations embodied in critical articles and reviews. Printed in the United States of America. For reproduction requests, comments, or corrections, please contact Artpeace Publishing/Liliana Kohann at ArtpeaceMusic@gmail.com

If you would like to order a copy of
A Thin Book of Fat Poems, or other products by Liliana, please visit www.LilianaKohann.com

Be kind to your future self...

a THIN BOOK of **Fat** POEMS

... and your future will be kind to you.

A NOTE TO THE READER

"The first and greatest victory is to conquer yourself."
—*Plato*

This book of poems came to life during the years 1999 to 2004, a difficult period in my life. During this time, I experienced a lot of disappointments, confusion, and pain. I was staying strong for others, yet at the same time I was becoming weaker and weaker within myself. Where once I was a happy, social, outgoing person, I had become someone who was more comfortable hiding, more comfortable staying invisible.

INVISIBLE ME

I lost my Self, somewhere during life.
My body seemed to be the only thing that survived...

As a committed mother, I was raising three little sons the best I could, essentially by myself. Raising children was a huge joy for me; it was never a problem. After all, the love for my children is what kept me going, but in some way it also blinded me to what was really going on in my life and in my marriage. With time,

I was beginning to realize the damage my then-husband's behavior was causing in my life and my children's lives. I was enduring pain that a young mother should never have to endure.

This book, however, is not about my pain. It is about my transition from pain to healing and growth.

Most of the poems in this book were written in the middle of the night. Something within was waking me up around 2:00 a.m. and prodding me to write in my journal. A lot of my writing was coming out in the form of poems. These poems to me were like miracles. They were different, unlike any poems I had written before. Whether it was Divine inspiration, my subconscious, or simply my desire to get better, these poems took the form of an inner coach, an inner healer. They seemed to provide me with a roadmap of what I needed to change in my life, and, at the same time, to give me the right and permission to fully experience and express the pain or any other emotion I was feeling.

So today I allowed myself to cry.
I don't have to be embarrassed of my tears.
I don't need to justify my reasons.
And oh, how good it feels...

Giving myself that right was a big step in my own healing. These poems helped me grasp the great wisdom in emotions. Whether it was fear, sadness, self-disappointment, longing, wanting to give up—even making fun of myself—all was allowed. So many people tell us to get rid of our emotions, or to let them pass through us. I feel sad when I hear that. Emotions can be used as great gifts that help us grow.

You can see this demonstrated beautifully in the Pixar movie *Inside Out*. True joy comes only when true sadness is allowed to speak, when it is no longer suppressed but rather is allowed to be fully expressed.

Creativity often follows. In my case, humorous poems and characters kept appearing in my mind, including the lady that you see on the cover of this book. This is how *The Thin Book of Fat Poems* came to life.

One of my favorite poems is *Who's Fault Is It, Really?*, which I wrote in 2003. It is a conversation between different body parts, each trying to find out who is to blame for eating too many jelly beans. Eventually, Brain blames it on Emotion. Stomach then yells at Emotion to go away...

...but Emotion rustled softly,
twisted, turned and hissed this sound:
"I would gladly disappear,
but first, please, I must be found!"

Tears and laughter can feed the hunger of one's soul much faster than food.

I'd like to clarify that my use of the word "fat" in this book's title actually refers to much more than the stuff that gets stuck around our waists. Taking full advantage of poetic license, I use the word "fat" to represent any unnecessary weight one carries by oneself, or puts unnecessarily on others. This unhealthy, slowly-killing-us emotional, physical, and spiritual residue is a weight we were never designed to carry.

It is unresolved guilt, un-faced fear, misplaced shame and unexpressed anger. It is an un-lived dream and un-used potential. It is invalid criticism from others that has now become your own, and like a heinous creature, or a broken record it repeats inside your head its wicked mantra: "You are not good for anything!" But in actuality, you are good for much more than you can even imagine.

…it is not your weakness
it is your Uniqueness.

If you struggle with weight, it is highly likely that you have bottled up your emotions. Once you allow them to flow freely, you are creating more room within you for objectivity, understanding, and compassion toward yourself. You are more vulnerable, open, and honest with yourself. It is from there that you will gain clarity; your attempts to lose weight, overcome procrastination, conquer addiction, or make other positive changes will then be much easier. It will make sense to you. It will not be a painful chore, but a playful, enriching journey.

…No longer room for stones
But soil fertile and soft
Where flowers like me can grow
Where we can cherish it all
Where we all can become
The heroes we were meant to be.

I can only hope that these poems, funny or serious, will help you, like they helped me, befriend and learn from your emotions, and find the courage to face what you need to face and the hope to proceed no matter what—or maybe simply help you notice YOU. If not, at least we will have a few good laughs.

Let's go on this journey together,
We were never meant to be alone.
We will share, laugh and cry,
And our troubles will shortly be gone.

Happy Travels

a THIN Book of **Fat** Poems

POEMS *and* DRAWINGS

by

LILIANA KOHANN

a THIN Book of **Fat** Poems

My Supper and Three Desserts

My supper and three desserts
I just ate.
         And ate,
                  and ate.

And now I am ready to plan
How to lose all this weight.

And I better do it fast,
Before I get hungry again.

'Cause, you see,
When Hunger comes

It may also eat my plan!

I Can Love Myself, *but...*

I can love myself,
>but...

There are some exceptions
>to this rule:

When there is a box of chocolates
>in front of me,

Or if I behave
>like a fool,

Or if I make the same mistake
>twice,

Or if someone's name
>I can't memorize,

Or when I get lazy
>or when I am late,

Or if I can't keep the promises
>I made,

Or eat the wrong foods,
>or procrastinate,

Or I don't say the right things,
	or gain too much weight,

I guess I can only love myself
	when I'm perfect

		and great!

A Choice

I choose pralines and cream
over a good body

I choose Fig Newtons
over my success

I choose cookie dough
over healthy teeth

I choose chocolate
over prayer and rest

I choose sweets
over friends

I choose weakness
over strength

I choose sugar and him
over my happiness

I choose his ambivalence
over love

I choose his indifference
over my inner voice

I choose to support
the sugar producers of the world

They are the best
That's what they say

They make me feel good
five minutes a day

I choose those five minutes
over long peaceful nights

I choose my destruction
over poems to write

I choose my false statement
that one day I'll be strong

I choose my so-called husband
over writing songs

I choose tears and hiding
over lighting my way

Bare survival and darkness
over sunny days

I choose chocolate truffles
over my own poise

Gentle whispers of meadows?
I choose chaos and noise!

I choose constant failure
over cherishing my skills

Sugar will kill me?
I choose to be killed!

What great choices I'm making
yet still I wonder why

Despite these great choices
I consider myself... bright!

I am so educated
so well read and smart

I have great common sense
a compassionate heart

There is only one flaw
that I guess I can't see

That this sense and compassion
can't be turned toward me.

Fear

Such fear has overtaken me now
A fear bigger than my heart

It is so present here
That its heartbeat I hear

Its presence takes over
Everything around

My world, my dreams
And I... can't be found

I disappear
In the face of fear

And I don't know why
I can't look into its eye

Maybe I sense death...
Or maybe I fear

That once fear is gone
    I...
       would have to

              APPEAR.

Death of a Lover

Your coldness became
        too cold

your ego
        too proud

your indifference
        too poignant

your silence
        too loud

your emptiness
        too shallow

your selfishness
        too clear

your lack of love
        too obvious

your backbone
        too sheer

your presence
                too distant

your carelessness
                too deep

your ignorance
                too secure

your heart
                too cheap

my love became
                too lost

my self-esteem
                too sad

your comments
                too cruel

my protection
                too fat

your judgments

too LOUD

my own voice

way

too

low

your reactions
        too fast

my heartbeat
        too slow

    my heartbeat

        too
            slow...

            t o o
                s l o w . . .

              t o o
                  s l o w . . .

Two Creatures

Oh, I am SO talented,

and so many things I know.

I can do THIS,

        I can do THAT,

but the problem is

        —I DON'T!

But it is not my fault, really.
This I swear.

        It is them,

the two wicked creatures
who live here.

They're the ones

who bring

this SHAME!

And I always struggle with them,
as one makes me work
> A LOT.

Everything must be perfect,
and it is a waste
> IF NOT!

Yet the other wicked creature
tells me how deprived she feels

Of all the fun, friends and laughter,
and how we waste

> **ALL**

> **HER**

> **SKILLS!**

So I argued,

and I quarreled,

tried to get them

out of sight.

But it never worked until I
really listened to my heart.

And I finally understood
that they are a part of me,

And since one must live with creatures,
learn to live with them must he.

So instead of fighting with them,
I began to learn their ways,

And I listened to their needs,
and what they both had to say.

FINALLY...

there was no quarrel,

just a friendly,

charming chat,

and I was surprised how easily,

all my problems

were worked out:

"Oh, I am so overwhelmed
with all the things
that I must do.

Can you help me just a little?"
asked one creature.
"Please, can you?"

"Yes, I can," said the other,
"but when all the things are done,
will you help me?"

"Help with what?"

"With just having

LOTS OF FUN!"

So when you have

TOO MUCH to do,

and you don't know
where to start,

just sit down,
and really listen,

To the CREATURES in

your HEART.

I Ate Too Many *of* These

I ate too many of these,

and too many of those.

Now I feel so disgusted,

and fed up—

up to

my nose!

ADDICTION

Addiction is a terrible thing.
It makes your integrity shrink.

In fact it makes it so very small
That you believe it's not there at all.

Addiction is a toxic friend.
It knocks you down,
         then gives you its hand.

It pulls you up, and when you begin
To walk, it knocks you down again.

Addiction is a vicious thing.
It makes you believe that you're a king.

And just when you begin to rule
It laughs at you, " A king?! A fool!"

Addiction is a nasty leech.
It drinks your blood,
         your source of life.

But though a leech leaves
         when it gets full,

         Addiction stays
                  until you die.

Simply Free

For me I want to be
free

for them I want to be
one of them

for her I want to be
a hero

for him I want to be
stress-free

for all of them
I want to be

everyone
but me

But for me
I want to be

simply

FREE

The Most Stubborn Thing

The most stubborn THING
I ever knew

is the weight
stuck to my body.

No matter what
I say or do

it sits right here,
fearing nobody.

I say, "Please,"
it says, "NO."

I say, "Leave,"
it won't go.

I say, "I really
don't want you here,"

and in more places
it appears!

I say,
"I hate you, go away."

It says,
"But I intend to stay."

And every day
we have this war,

and out of frustration
I eat even more!

Such a stubborn THING
is this weight on my body

so mean and ruthless,
fearing nobody.

And when I try to say,

"But you don't look so good,"

it quickly says,

"Who cares?!"

and makes me eat

more food!

And when I really beg,

"Please, please go away,"

It retorts rather swiftly,

"Shut up, and pass the cake."

And I hate to admit

but I do what it says,

this nasty, stubborn

THING

stuck around my waist.

I Succeeded

They say one must believe
to succeed,

but if that's true,
how is it that

I didn't believe
I would gain weight,

yet still I succeeded

—I'm **Fat!**

BIG O!

"Oh, no!"
said Big O.

"Look what
happened
to me:

I've lost weight
and I look great

But they still
prefer to look
at X, and Y
and Z!

Oh, no!

Oh, no!"
said Big O

and made
a longing sigh

But then
it thought

for a while...

And it said,

"It's not so bad,

at least

I look like

I."

Through the Eyes of a Loving Mother

Through the eyes of a loving mother
I am no longer
                the lazy one

I am doing enough as it is
As a matter of fact
                I deserve more fun

Through the eyes of a loving mother
Extra pounds?
                I don't have to lose

I am pretty attractive as I am
I can lose a few pounds...
                if I choose

Through the eyes of a loving mother
I am not clumsy
                and slow

I am faster than many others
And I'm learning at just
                the right flow

Through the eyes of a loving mother
I am not a failure,
                    oh, no

I just chose the road less traveled
And I chose to walk
                    on my own

Through the eyes of a loving mother
I am not stubborn
                    or proud

I'm persistent, caring for others
And I speak my own truth
                    aloud

Through the eyes of a loving mother
I am not wasting
                    my life

On the contrary, I'm living it fully,
Into the deepest waters
                    I dive

Through the eyes of a loving mother
I am not naive
                or blind

I'm not selfish, or controlling either.
I am open,
                giving and kind

But I've never been looked at with those eyes
Till one day I was
                struck with awe

In the eyes of my child... a reflection...
What a loving mother
                I saw!

Through the eyes of that loving mother
Everything looks so pretty
                and I

Choose to look at myself from now on
Through only my own

                truly loving eyes.

I Took Something Away

Today is my birthday
but it is an unusual day

Instead of giving
something to myself

I took
something AWAY

I usually would
give myself sweets

As many as I could eat
but today I didn't

Instead I asked
what do I
      really need

Do I need those extra
heavy pounds

Making me sick
and slow?

Do I need more
because it's my birthday

Or do I need to
let them go?

So instead of giving
myself something

For my birthday
my special day

I walked, I danced
and I worked out

And I took
one pound
        AWAY.

$$2 + 2 + 4 + 8 + 2 + 11 = ?$$

If I Could Eat Only Two

If I could eat only TWO

it would be absolutely great.

But no, I can't...

I first eat TWO,
then TWO again,
then FOUR,
then EIGHT.

Then only TWO
after supper,
and then ELEVEN
before the bath.

Oh well, at least
I'm getting better
at my MATH!

Whose Fault Is It, Really?

As my Mouth greedily crunches
these chocolate jelly beans,
my poor, over-exhausted Stomach

   begs,

      pleads,

         moans,

            and screams,

"You selfish, disgusting Mouth Hole,
  how could you be so mean?!

  Can't you see?

     I'm sick and tired,

        of those

          chocolate

             jelly beans."

"Well, I do enjoy them but
I hope that you understand,
it is not my fault, really,

    It is
        this
            Lady's
                Hand."

"Hand! How dare you be so cruel!"
yelled my Stomach, but in vain.

"It's not me," Hand replied.

    "It is
        this
            Lady's
                Brain!"

"Aha, Brain, you wrinkled traitor!
Well, at least *you* should know
that eating so many beans
is not good,

    so stop
        that
            flow!"

But my Brain calmly answered,
"I am not the one to blame.
There's a lost creature here
and EMOTION is her name."

"Well, EMOTION, go away!
 You destroy me, can't you see?

 I don't want to eat

 those

 beans.

 They are not good for me!"

But EMOTION rustled softly,

 twisted,

 turned

 and hissed

 this sound,

"I would gladly disappear,
 but first, please,

I must be found!"

a THIN Book of Fat Poems

Here are some excerpts from my journal that I wrote right before the following poem, *Today I Allowed Myself To Cry:*

From my journal, 2002

*Tears are what let one's guard down.
Tears allow us to be ourselves.
Tears are like water that pours out of
a spring and carves a river. With that
river the pain is carried away, and
therefore tears are what allow us
to be pain free.*

*Today I allowed myself to cry
without limits, without any judgments.
Oh, how good it is to feel the tears falling
down, to feel the freedom of allowing
myself to be who I really am. How good it
is to feel each tear carrying out a bit of my
pain, a pain that was held way too long, a pain
that was kept in secret, like an undocumented alien
forced into hiding.*

*How good it is to let myself cry even if
there are many people who have it
much worse. How good it is to feel my
pain, and not feel guilty about feeling it.
Yes...*

Today I Allowed Myself to Cry

Today I allowed myself to cry.
I don't have to be embarrassed of my tears.
I don't need to justify my reasons.
And oh, how good it feels.

I let them fall as they come,
As the cloud allows the rain,
And I feel their heaviness flowing out
As they carry out my pain.

How good it feels to cry,
And to know that it is my right,
After all, it's the only way
For my sorrow to be truly out;

For my pain to be resolved,
For my mind to become clear.
If Nature never let the rain fall
      how would
            the clouds
                  disappear?

Unfair War

I lost a war!
But it was not fair.

See, my opponent
Cannot even think.

I just can't believe it,
I have been defeated

By such a tiny,
Little thing!

And I thought for hours,
Trying various tactics,

Struggling and
Sweating to win,

While this tiny cookie
Just sat on the counter,

Not even
      cracking a grin!

If Perfect I Could Be

If perfect I could be
I would be so good to me
I would be so happy
And so pleased
        with me.

I'd make perfect speeches
I would only do what's best
People would admire me
I would hardly need
        to rest.

I wouldn't eat junk
I'd make no mistakes
I'd never talk too much
I'd give what
        it takes.

I would make my living
Doing what I love to do
I'd pray every night
I'd always
        be true.

I'd solve every problem
I'd help everyone
I'd be a perfect mother
I'd have
              a perfect son.

I'd always be peaceful
Never sad or depressed
I would be spontaneous
I would sing
              the best.

I'd have a healthy body
I'd do nothing in vain
Failure would not know me
I would not know
              pain.

I would have perfect vision...

Oh, how nice it'd be to SEE
How my flaws and faults
Perfectly
              perfect me.

Before and After

I got inspired by *Before* and *After*
Pictures of those who were fat.
And I decided to go on a diet,
And take some pictures like that.

BEFORE

And here they are:
>   *Before*—I looked so fat.
>   On the diet, I looked so thin!
>   And now...
>   What the heck is THAT?
>   It is *After* and
>   I look just like *Before*—
>   >   FAT!

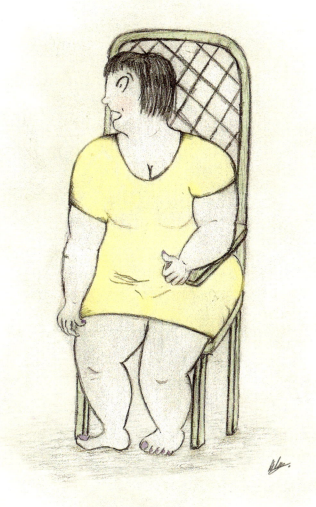

AFTER

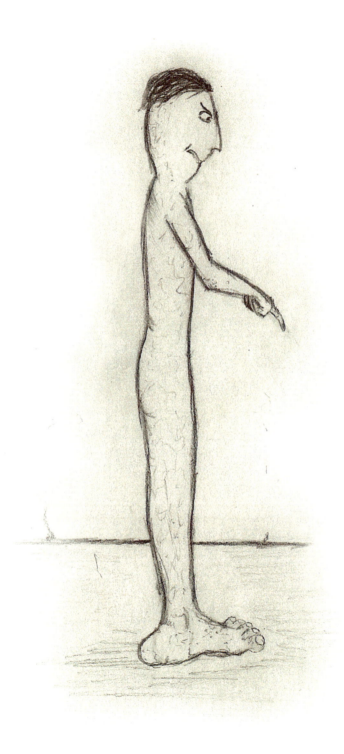

I Have an Enemy

I have an Enemy.

Whenever I decide
to walk outside,
my Enemy says,

"Why bother,
　stay inside."

Whenever I desire
to light my fire,
my Enemy says,

"Oh, wait now,
　you're too tired."

Whenever I've concluded
I need to become rooted,
my Enemy says,

"Keep floating,
　you have been excluded."

Whenever I would vow,
"I won't eat sweets," somehow
my Enemy reminds me,

"But it's your birthday now."

Whenever I would say,
"I'm starting my new way,"
my Enemy would whisper,

"Tomorrow, not today."

    So with style and a rhyme,
    I failed most of the time.
    And the good American pie
    we waste, my Enemy and I.

Till   one   day

    Death   knocked

        at   my   door...

My Enemy said with a smile,

    "Get up and go, bye, bye.
    It is your time to leave;
    It is your time to die."

Obediently,
    like a little kid

I listened,
    as I always did.

And with my
    head down

I started
    to proceed.

But right before
I turned the knob on the door,
I stood up really tall
and said to my Enemy,

    "NO! You go!"

Then to my surprise
my Enemy did arise
and said,

"Yes, master."

And then

    slowly

        walked

            OUTside.

In shock I never knew,
I stood for

        a minute

            or two.

Well, bye, bye my Enemy,

Now, I've got things

      TO DO!

I Lost My Self

I lost my Self,
Somewhere during life.
My Body seemed to be
The only thing that survived.

And It kept on searching
All around the world,
Asking friends and strangers,
If they'd seen Its soul.

It so much believed
That someone would know
The right place, and direction
Toward which to go.

Even though It found
Different souls and hearts,
It just became weaker…
None of them were right.

Yet people kept on sending It
On different fruitless paths.

Now my worn-out body,
On my bed It lies.

One day It rose to leave,
By the door It stood.

It said with a frail voice,
The very best It could,

"I can't live any longer,
So it is goodbye."

It was in this very moment
That I closed my eyes.

I remembered a little girl,
In pain, in shame, neglected,

Vulnerable, sensitive, alone,
Not heard... disconnected.

And I felt compassion for her;
I understood her pain, her life.

I held her and listened to her,
Gave her time, let her cry.

And as I did, I felt the reunion.
The girl that sat by my side

Held my hand. I saw her smiling.
Something was shifting inside.

I started feeling the heartbeat within...
I slowly opened my eyes.

"My dear Body," I softly whispered.
"I am your Soul, your Heart."

My Body heard me, came to life,
And swiftly turned around.

"Ah, I found you," rejoiced my Body.
"Yes, you did. Finally, we all are found!"

And still to this day, we live happily:
The Girl, my Body, my Soul,

For there's a new friend
That lives with us now;

    It is

        COMPASSION

            that connects us all.

I Run For...

Some people run for exercise,
Some for other causes,
Like for cancer cures
Or for osteoporosis.

And I do believe
That all this running is good.
But, I made it simple,
I run—for FOOD.

My Uniqueness

It's not my weakness,
it is my openness.

It's not my doubts,
it is my questioning mind.

It's not that I say too much,
it is my courage to share.

It's not my fear,
it is my prudence.

It's not my stupidity,
it is my choice of what I
want to know.

It's not my credulity,
it is my trust.

It's not my depression,
it is my acceptance.

It's not my recklessness,
it is my curiosity,
and love of life.

It's not my chaos,
it is my artistic soul.

It's not my weakness,
it is my
        UNIQUENESS.

THE MIRROR THOUGHT

The mirror thought:

"God, she is so beautiful, so talented
Gentle, loving and smart
She is so gracious, humble and giving
The brightest star in my night.

She is so gifted, and so creative
Oh, what a pretty sight
Look how she cares for all God's creatures
Look how she carries His light.

She is so fun, and so attractive
I love her sweet, caring eyes
She is so tender, and so accepting
And yes, so very wise.

She's like a child, sweet and vulnerable
Daring to go to the end
She's the greatest teacher, and mother
The greatest soulmate and friend.

But the one thing I can't understand...
Why can't she see
Any of those beautiful things
When she
             is looking
                          at me?"

My Two Halves

One half of me　　　　the other half
feels so happy,　　　　so sad.

One half of me　　　　the other one
wants to give,　　　　to possess.

One half of me　　　　The other half
so much in pain,　　　ready to laugh,
depression keeps　　　a queen with
her down.　　　　　　a golden crown.

One half of me　　　　the other lives
lives for me,　　　　　for others.

One half is　　　　　　the other—
a lost child,　　　　　a searching mother.

One half of me　　　　The other half
wants to be　　　　　remains in shadow,
a star that shines　　keeps hiding
for all.　　　　　　　from the world.

One half of me   The other one
is so courageous,   lives in terror
will do whatever   of failures
it takes.   and mistakes.

One half of me   the other
wants to give up,   will always try.

One half of me   the other
lives for the truth,   lives in a lie.

And there were times when it was hard
to live with those halves like that,
especially the one that would get down,
depressed, fearful or sad.

But not any longer.

Now I love them.

A sense of peace finally arrived
once I understood,
that both sides

are good,

and both are mine for life.

Once I Burn Away

I will be OK
Once I burn away
All the crap
That I eat
Each and every day.

Wait, who says
That I am not OK now?
I am! I just don't fit
In my pants
         somehow.

I Want But I Won't

I want to eat this chocolate
But I'm telling you
I won't
You can take it, you can leave it
Doesn't matter
'Cause I won't.

I have told you
I'm not lying
I will not eat it now
So don't even try to tempt me
I won't put it
In my mouth.

I won't even
Try to taste it
Not even a tiny bit
I won't look at it or smell it
I will not!
I will not eat!

Oops, my hand!
It didn't hear me
It is grabbing... no, no, please!
My mouth also
Didn't listen
And there goes the whole big piece.

I just can't believe
It happened
Well, next time I swear I won't
I won't even
Talk about it
I may want to, but I won't!

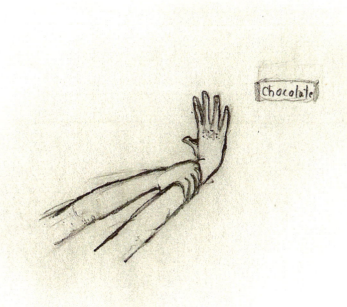

I'm Choosing the Change

I live as if I were
afraid
      to be noticed.

I walk making sure
I don't touch
      the dirt.

I laugh as if I were
afraid of
      being funny.

And I talk as if I were
afraid to
      be heard.

I dance in slow motion
as if I were
      ashamed.

I breathe in the air
as if it were
      not mine.

I hide my emotions
as if they were
      illegal.

I disguise my passions
as if they were
      a crime.

I live my own life
as a slave
      to death.

Something is not right,
something foreign,
      strange.

But I'm changing
      NOW,

I am in control.

My life is my song.
I'm choosing the

      CHANGE

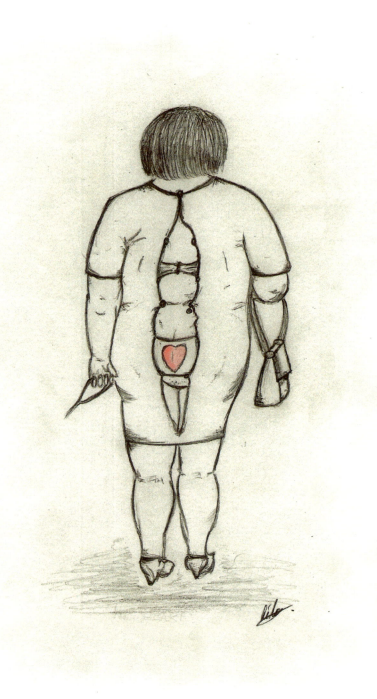

Happy Valentine's

First I used to wear size seven,
Then up to size nine,
Then I went to eleven,
And now—I don't even count.

I finally decided,
No more new dresses or pants.
No matter how much I gain,
I've got to fit in what I have.

And I feel bound to admit that
Sometimes I have to work hard.
Like today, when I put on my old dress
And my panties with a Valentine's heart.

Yet, I must have looked pretty good,
Since people were staring my way.
I only wonder what this one guy meant
When I heard him say,

"Thank you, Ma'am,

your HEART made my day!"

First I Must Wait

First
I must wait
until I
lose weight.

I would like to
dance with friends,
and go out to the lake,
meet some more people
who will inspire me,
but first
      I must get in shape!

Yeah, I would like to
play volleyball,
and maybe join a club,
go out hiking,
enjoy the fresh air,
but first
      I must lose this flab!

Oh, the ocean
sounds so tempting,
I would listen to its sounds.
I would love to walk barefooted
upon the golden sand
but first
        I must lose these pounds!

But to tell you the truth
I am pretty tired
of all this waiting I do.

        Why am I waiting?
        What am I scared of?
        What is the real truth?

"Nothing in nature disappears."
That must be
        what gives me a scare.

Where will my pounds go
if I lose them,
and what will appear,
        and where?

What if the NEW me
would suddenly appear,
as evolved as
        a muse?

I would then have to do
what now I dream,
and I won't have an excuse.

I could take a risk,
and I could believe
that I have all that it takes,
I could do it,
and I will do it
but first (oh, no!)

    I must get in shape.

Hopes Up High

We like to eat pecan pie,
my friends and I.
We like to talk,
and go for a walk,
and keep our hopes up high.

We keep them ^{HIGH}
so no one can
reach them and see.

The problem is...
neither can we.

My Mind Is Brilliant

My Mind is brilliant.
It knows everything I need.
It knows where and how to live,
What to buy,
               what to read.

It knows how to reach my dream,
Every tiny point it covers.
My Mind makes fantastic plans,
And great methods
               it discovers.

My Mind knows what's the best,
Where and whom I should meet.
How to lose all my weight,
What to eat and
               not to eat.

My Mind knows precisely what
I should do when I'm shy,
How to get my job done well.
My Mind knows.
               Well, but I…

Also have this Body here,
Very stubborn and unkind,
Mostly does the opposite
Of my great,
          all-knowing Mind!

When my Mind says, "*Right* is good,"
My Body says, "Yep, I know,
But today *left* feels better,
So today
          left I go."

When my Mind says, "Follow me,
I wrote this fantastic plan.
It will make your dreams come true,
You will be
          in shape again."

My Body says, "Yep, I know.
Maybe I will try some day
But right now I'm really tired.
I think I will
          pass today."

When my Mind, in its mind,

Creates a healthful meal,
My Body says, "Sounds so good!
But that's not
        what I feel."

Yet somehow, by some strange force,
My Body goes to the store,
And buys the wrong foods.

    "Stop it now!" my Mind yells.

And my Body buys
        some more!

Now, it's 3:00 in the morning
And my Body wants to sleep.
But my Brilliant Mind is working,
My Body is
        getting weak.

"Please, dear Mind, let me rest,"
This time my weak Body pleads.
But my Mind says, "No, I won't."
And it thinks…
        and it reads…

So now I begin to wonder
Who is really the guilty one?
My stubborn, rebellious Body
Or my
        too-demanding Mind?

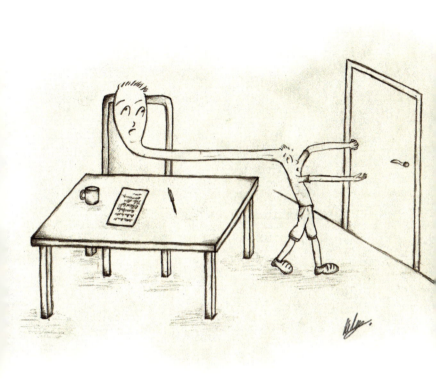

"Please, dear Mind, go to sleep,"
Asks my Body, "I'm so tired."

"Yep, I know, but I won't!"

Well then, sorry, but

        YOU'RE FIRED!

If Sometimes It's Too Much

If sometimes there is a problem
you can't get out of your way,
you have tried everything,
but the trouble won't go away...

You've been trying for so long,
yet nothing is working for you,
and you just want to

GIVE UP,

but the world tells you, "No, don't!"

Sometimes I say

"Please, do."

Give it up,

lie down,

and watch what you

GAVE UP

floating UP like a helium balloon,

out of your mind,

out of your house,

above the trees,

above the clouds,

above the moon,

beyond the planets,

above the stars,

up and UP,

out of your reach,

above the sky,

and now... you can't see

what you gave up.

Yes, it is gone and forgotten.
The sky just looks so clear and blue
and now the only thing you see
is the golden sun shining

FOR YOU

A Thin Book of Fat Poems

I Could've Been a Star

I could've been a star,
I really could.
I had the hips,
I had the boobs.
I could've been a star,
I really could
If only I
Had eaten the food
That I should've.
But I couldn't,

It didn't taste
      that good.

BURDEN OF CHOICE

Every day a little Voice
Says I do have a choice,
Close the windows, open doors,
Right, or left,
      the choice is yours.

How I wish that Voice would say
"You should choose *this* today."
Or that It could make me see
What's the best
      choice for me.

But it doesn't let me know
And since I reap what I sow,
Well maybe "sow" I could
But I don't know
    if I should:

Start with a great attitude,
Eat just good, healthy food,
Or feel down, and depressed,
Eat junk food, and have
    a rest?

Selfish is that little Voice
And my failures—it enjoys.
Selfish is that little Voice
That tells me—

    I have the choice.

COMPETITIVE DIETER

My friends want to know
why, when I'm on a diet

I feel so fulfilled
and great.

So here I am
revealing my secret—

what I do
when I want to lose weight.

I absolutely
refuse to be

like others
who failed before.

One diet is not
good enough for me,

I've got to do better
and MORE!

I go on THREE diets
at the same time
and I eat them together,
just like that:

one high in carbs,

the second high in protein

and the third one

high in **FAT**!

What Would It Take?

What would it take
to remove my attention
from these tempting
sweets?

What could be more soothing
than the calming feeling
of melting milk chocolate
in my mouth?

What could be more intimate
than crunching
these sweet pecan pralines
between my teeth?

What could be more secure
than that feeling

of peace,

of satisfaction,

of contentment,

of this sweet DI*S*TRAC*T*ION?

What would it have to be,
to take my attention off
these slowly-enticing-me
sweets?

A lover?
A man?
A person?
A friend?

A caring, loving

hand.

The Real Beauty

It's April 10
it's 2:00 a.m.
I jump in front of the mirror
to have a little chat
with my fat,
as I used to do when I couldn't sleep.
But today I didn't say the usual thing to it,
which was,
"I hate you, fat!
How dare you stick to me like that?"
Today I saw myself through different eyes.
Today I jumped with joy.
The fat looked the same
but instead of cursing it,
feeling its pain,
I looked straight into its many eyes
and I squeezed it with love,
and pinched it too.
Then I looked at it proudly,
and I said,
"Oh, my dear fat, look at the beauty
underneath you!"

It Was Not My Dream

It was not my dream
it was just an illusion
of happiness

It was not my plan
it was just a bunch of
unrelated circumstances

It was not my will
it was just my surrender
to the pressures outside

It was not my voice
it was just an echo
of those who never tried

It was not my choice
it was just a mere motion
to please others

It was not my life
it was just a reflection
of what was expected

It was not my song
it was just a karaoke version of
an unmet expectation

It was not *my* dream...

And now I want
    my plan,
    my will,
    my voice,
    my choice,
    my life,
    my song,
and my dream back.

The time has come.

Which Child In Me?

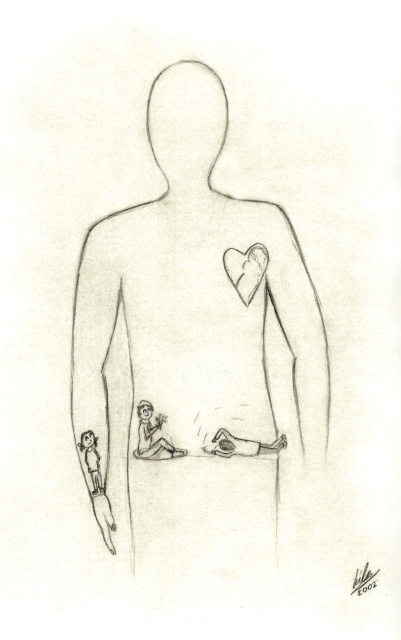

One child in me
wants cookies now,
and even though I don't really want them,
this child will make me
eat them somehow.

One child in me
just wants to play,
and even though I want to work,
this child will make me
waste my day.

Now, which child in me
so desperately needs my caress?
Even though I think I'm loving,
I just can't hear
what this child says.

Maybe if I could notice this child,
and listen to what she has to say,
cookies won't be needed for now,
and maybe I won't need to
waste my whole day.

But which child in me says,
"No! I'd rather curl up and pout!"
This child... pardon me,
will go for
               TIME OUT.

In My Desire For Satisfaction

In my desire for satisfaction
I do it all.
I think, I plan,
I imagine the end.
Yes, positive thinking
I do a lot.
I work on my faith,
Improve my ways,
And reprogram my
Every negative thought.
I do affirmations,
I work on my patience,
I reorganize and revise my plan.
I think of improvements,
Envision all movements,
And do it over, and over again.

But I am noticing something...
Strangely...
The things I want to do
Remain undone.
So what's the conclusion?

That in my desire for satisfaction
I do it all

but

    the

        ACTION

Who Would?

I would be so relieved,
I would feel so good
If someone would
Just take this food!

But nobody does.
So therefore I must
Sit and eat all this food
'Cause I just can't
Throw it away!
Who would?

My Therapist Said

My therapist said,
In order for me to grow,
I must get to the BOTTOM of my addiction,
And that's the only way to go.

He said it may take up to a year,
But I didn't want to wait.
Once I got home I started right away,
And boy, did I do great!

First I got to the bottom of the fridge,
Then to the middle of it,
Then cleared off the top shelf.
What a great job I did!

Surely not a year, not even a day,
And I'm already at the top!
And I am really proud to say,
I grew! A LOT!

The Two of Me

Whenever I fail,
or say something wrong,

Eat too much
or spill some tea,

I immediately feel
the pressure inside,

I get embarrassed
and get mad
       —at me.

"You have to get off your own back,"
said my good friend, Marie.

And thus I learned why
I felt so heavy:

I've been carrying

the TWO OF ME.

Two Small Words

God, I can't get myself to do anything.
      I CAN'T. Why is that?
    I just sit in my chair
        or lie
              in bed.

   I hate
         the way
                  I feel today!

I don't know why.
I don't work, don't rest
don't laugh
        don't cry.

I am paralyzed with some
alien emotion
that creates in me this
stagnant
        de-motion.

God, I don't know
what to do or why.
I guess I'll just lie
       and lie
              and lie…

I am lying and waiting
nothing is changing
nothing is moving
or
       re-arranging.

The sun isn't shining
the rain isn't falling
nobody's coming
nobody's
       calling.

God, I don't know
what to say or do.
I guess I'll just lie
and wait for a miracle
       or two.

Suddenly from a distance
I hear a gentle knocking,
and then I hear
a clear voice
       talking,

"I wonder how long until you
realize that you are dead."

What did you say?

I'm dead??

"Yes, you are dead.
No more sadness, tears
No more disappointments
No more clouds
     and fears.

No embarrassing moments
No failure, no distance
No indifference, no coldness
No doubts
     no resistance.

No more *should* or *have to*
No more obligations,
No bills and debts
No guilt and
     no tension."

Wow, how great it feels!
I can just be.
Too bad that there is
     no more
          ME.

That realization suddenly hurts...

As I slowly wake up I realize
It was just a dream all along.

The voice that was talking
I no longer hear.

All *shoulds* and *have to's*

are back.

But with them hand in hand
are two small words and I

feel them

quite strongly:

I CAN

From my journal, 2004

I am beginning to notice myself...
I had this vision:
I was sitting somewhere in between Earth and the stars.
I was looking at one particular bright star.
Then I noticed that this star had a shadow.
In that shadow I saw...

In the Shadow of a Star

In the shadow of a star

there is a child

unnoticed.

In the shadow of a star

there are hidden tears.

There is someone neglected,

forgotten,

lost within the darkness,

in the night of fears.

As I slowly raise my hand

to greet the star,

from beneath the darkness

this child looks at me.

How it hurts,

this child forgotten...

How it hurts to see

what I see.

In the shadow of a star

I can see many things:

talent great as sunlight,

belittled to a spark,

many broken hopes,

unexpressed emotions,

cruel, searing memories,

buried in the dark.

As I look through my eyes,

all those things I see

are my own reflections,

yes, that's all they are.

What a sad awareness...

Yet if I look

through the Eyes Divine

in the shadow of a star,

there's nothing else

but another

        STAR.

You Can

You can dance when your soul desires to
or
you can remain idle
to please others.

You can let others live your life
or
you can live your life
yourself.

You can be a foolish slave
to life's circumstances
or
you can be a wise person
who uses life's circumstances
as a tool for growth
and betterment.

You can believe in yourself
or
you can believe others
not believing in you.

You can let your free spirit
carry you through the mountains
or

you can allow others
to keep your spirit
chained to the bottom of the valley.

You can accept the challenge of change
or
you can choose the comfort
of misery.

PREVAIL
in your own heart's desires,
as they will be often obscured
by the desires of others.

SIMPLIFY
your life
as chaos will destroy you.

FOCUS
on your path
as you will be pulled astray.

WORK
persistently toward your dream
a little bit each day.

You CAN.

Hope

Life on earth is confusion
Happiness is a distant illusion
Hope is a tiny grain of sand
Yet it is here right in my hand

I open my palm slowly
And all that I see
Is this one grain of sand
From some faraway sea

All of me wants to quit
No strength to go on

Yet to this one small seed of hope

I choose to

hold on.

About the Joy

Of course I should write
about the Joy,
since for fifteen years
only darkness I knew.
Of course I should write
about the Joy,
with the hope that one day
you will feel it too:
multi-dimensional,
above and beyond,
purple and yellow

    it simply astounds!

INDEX

About the Joy, 148
Addiction, 38
Before and After, 70
Big O!, 48
Burden of Choice, 114
Choice, A, 18
Competitive Dieter, 116
Death of a Lover, 124
Fear, 23
First I Must Wait, 99
Happy Valentine's, 97
Hope, 146
Hopes Up High, 102
I Ate Too Many of These, 36
I Can Love Myself, But…, 16
I Could've Been a Star, 113
I Have an Enemy, 73
I Lost My Self, 78
I Run For…, 83
I Succeeded, 47
I Took Something Away, 54
I Want but I Won't, 92
It Was Not My Dream, 122
I'm Choosing the Change, 94
If I Could Eat Only Two, 57
If Perfect I Could Be, 68

If Sometimes It's Too Much, 108
In the Shadow of a Star, 141
In My Desire for Satisfaction, 126
Mirror Thought, The, 86
Most Stubborn Thing, The, 42
My Mind Is Brilliant, 104
My Supper and Three Desserts, 15
My Therapist Said, 131
My Two Halves, 88
My Uniqueness, 84
Oh, Well..., 155
Once I Burn Away, 91
Real Beauty, The, 121
Simply Free, 40
Through the Eyes of a Loving Mother, 50
Today I Allowed Myself to Cry, 65
Two Creatures, 28
Two of Me, The, 133
Two Small Words, 134
Unfair War, 67
What Would it Take?, 118
Which Child in Me?, 124
Who Would?, 129
Whose Fault Is It, Really?, 58
You Can, 144

Share & Stay Connected

If there is anything you want to share with us or with Liliana, or if you'd like to purchase additional books, you can write to Artpeace Publishing at
ArtpeaceMusic@gmail.com

To stay connected, get news, read more or listen to Liliana's music, visit her website:
www.LilianaKohann.com

More of Liliana's Healing Poems can be found in her Online Literary Journal,
The Healing Poems at
www.TheHealingPoems.com

Acknowledgments

I wish to thank Scott Greer, Ph.D., Lenna Wagner, Joe Newgarden, Chris and Katie Bradds, Jim Dineen, Halina Orzel, Linda Leftwitch, Ph.D., Clare "Lala" Glass, and my three wonderful sons, Julian, Adrian, and Thomas, for their ongoing love and support.

I'd also like to express my great gratitude to Bryan Hidalgo for all of his input, encouragement, and editorial advice from the inception of this project to its conclusion.

Lastly, I especially wish to extend my deepest appreciation to Franciszek Penczek for his tremendous faith in me, and the great support he provided for me and this project. I am eternally grateful.

OH, WELL...

Oh, well, what can I say?
I could write about it all day,
But I finished all the chocolates
So now I have nothing left to eat,

    and therefore...

        nothing to say.